The Wicked Book

of

KNOCK KNOCK
JOKES

The Wicked Book
of
KNOCK KNOCK JOKES

p

This is a Parragon Book
This edition published in 2002

Parragon
Queen Street House
4 Queen Street
Bath BA1 1HE, UK

Produced by Magpie Books, an imprint of
Constable & Robinson Ltd, London

ISBN 0-75255-040-3

A copy of the British Library Cataloguing-in-Publication Data
is available from the British Library

Printed and bound in the EC

Introduction

Knock Knock.
Who's there?
Sonia.
Sonia who?
Sonia shoe – and it stinks.

And there are masses more where that one came from. We've searched far and wide for rare ones, paid enormous sums of money for antique ones, snapped up a few fashionable ones and dug some up from under the bed. They're all here so get knocking and start giggling.

Knock Knock.
Who's there?
Abba.
Abba who?
Abba'out turn!
Quick march!

Knock Knock.
Who's there?
Abel.
Abel who?
Abel to see you, ha, ha!

Knock knock.
Who's there?
Ada.
Ada who?
Ada lot for breakfast.

Knock Knock.
Who's there?
Adam.
Adam who?
Adam will burst any minute now.

Knock Knock.
Who's there?
Adder.
Adder who?
Adder you get in here?

Knock Knock.
Who's there?
Ahmed.
Ahmed who?
Ahmed a big mistake coming here!

Knock Knock.
Who's there?
Aida.
Aida who?
Aida whole village cos I'm a monster.

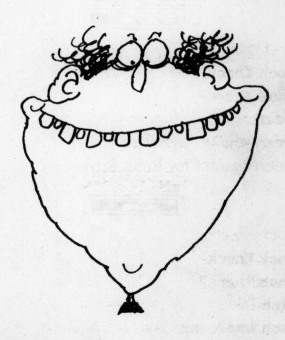

Knock Knock.
Who's there?
Aida.
Aida who?
Aida whole box of chocolates and I feel really sick.

Knock Knock.
Who's there?
Aileen.
Aileen who?
Aileen against my Rolls-Royce.

Knock Knock.
Who's there?
Aitch.
Aitch who?
Bless you.

Knock knock.
Who's there?
Al.
Al who?
Al be seeing you!

Knock Knock.
Who's there?
Alaska.
Alaska who?
Alaska one more time.

Knock Knock.
Who's there?
Aleta.
Aleta who?
Aleta bit of lovin'.

Knock Knock.
Who's there?
Alf.
Alf who?
Alf all if you don't catch me!

Knock Knock.
Who's there?
Alison.
Alison who?
Alison Wonderland.

Knock Knock.
Who's there?
Alma.
Alma who?
Almany times do I have to knock?

Knock Knock.
Who's there?
Althea.
Althea who?
Althea in court.

Knock knock.
Who's there?
Alvin.
Alvin who?
Alvin zis competition – just vait and see!

Knock knock.
Who's there?
Amanda.
Amanda who?
Amanda the table.

Knock knock.
Who's there?
Amber.
Amber who?
Amberter than I was yesterday.

Knock Knock.
Who's there?
Amin.
Amin who?
Amin man.

Knock Knock.
Who's there?
Ammonia.
Ammonia who?
Ammonia poor boy, nobody loves me.

Knock Knock.
Who's there?
Amos.
Amos who?
Amosquito.

Knock knock.
Who's there?
Amy.
Amy who?
Amy for the top.

Knock Knock.
Who's there?
Anais.
Anais who?
Anais cup of tea.

Knock Knock.
Who's there?
Anna.
Anna who?
Annather mosquito.

Knock knock.
Who's there?
Annabel.
Annabel who?
Annabel would be useful on this door.

Knock knock.
Who's there?
Annette.
Annette who?
Annette curtain looks good in the window.

Knock knock.
Who's there?
Annie.
Annie who?
Annie one you like.

Knock knock.
Who's there?
Anya.
Anya who?
Anya best behavior.

Knock Knock.
Who's there?
Apple.
Apple who?
Apple the door myself.

Knock Knock.
Who's there?
April.
April who?
April will make you feel better.

Knock Knock.
Who's there?
Armageddon.
Armageddon who?
Armageddon out of here quick.

Knock Knock.
Who's there?
Army Ant.
Army Ant who?
Army Ants coming for tea then?

Knock Knock.
Who's there?
Asia.
Asia who?
Asia mom in?

Knock Knock.
Who's there?
Atomic.
Atomic who?
Atomic ache is hard to stomach.

Knock Knock.
Who's there?
Attila.
Attila who?
Attila you no lies.

Knock Knock.
Who's there?
Augusta.
Augusta who?
Augusta wind will blow the witch away.

Knock Knock.
Who's there?
Austen.
Austen who?
Austentatiously rich.

Knock knock.
Who's there?
Aurora.
Aurora who?
Aurora's just come from a big lion!

Knock knock.
Who's there?
Ava.
Ava who?
Ava good mind to leave you.

Knock Knock.
Who's there?
Avenue.
Avenue who?
Avenue learned my name yet?

Knock Knock.
Who's there?
Avis.
Avis who?
Avisibly shaken person.

Knock Knock.
Who's there?
Baby Owl.
Baby Owl who?
Baby Owl see you later, baby not.

Knock Knock.
Who's there?
Bach.
Bach who?
Bach to work.

Knock Knock.
Who's there?
Bacon.
Bacon who?
Bacon a cake in the oven.

Knock knock.
Who's there?
Barbara.
Barbara who?
(sing) "Barbara black sheep, have you any wool?"

Knock Knock.
Who's there?
Bark.
Bark who?
Bark your car in the garage.

Knock Knock.
Who's there?
Basket.
Basket who?
Basket home, it's nearly dark.

Knock Knock.
Who's there?
Bat.
Bat who?
Bat you'll never guess!

Knock Knock.
Who's there?
Becker.
Becker who?
Becker the devil you know.

Knock Knock.
Who's there?
Bed.
Bed who?
Bed you can't guess who it is!

Knock Knock.
Who's there?
Bee.
Bee who?
Bee careful out there!

Knock Knock.
Who's there?
Beef.
Beef who?
Beef fair!

Knock Knock.
Who's there?
Belize.
Belize who?
Oh, Belize yourself then.

Knock knock.
Who's there?
Bella.
Bella who?
Bella the ball.

Knock Knock.
Who's there?
Belle.
Belle who?
Belle-t up and open the door.

Knock Knock.
Who's there?
Ben and Anna.
Ben and Anna who?
Ben and Anna split.

Knock Knock.
Who's there?
Ben Hur.
Ben Hur who?
Ben Hur an hour – let me in.

Knock Knock.
Who's there?
Benin.
Benin who?
Benin hell.

Knock Knock.
Who's there?
Berlin.
Berlin who?
Berlin maiden over.

Knock knock.
Who's there?
Bernadette.
Bernadette who?
Bernadette my dinner.

Knock Knock.
Who's there?
Bertha.
Bertha who?
Bertha day boy.

Knock knock.
Who's there?
Bethany.
Bethany who?
Bethany good shows recently?

Knock knock.
Who's there?
Bette.
Bette who?
Bette of roses.

Knock Knock.
Who's there?
Bhuto.
Bhuto who?
Bhuton the other foot.

Knock knock.
Who's there?
Bill.
Bill who?
Bill of rights.

Knock Knock.
Who's there?
Biro.
Biro who?
Biro light of the moon.

Knock Knock.
Who's there?
Bjork.
Bjork who?
Bjork in the USSR.

Knock Knock.
Who's there?
Blair.
Blair who?
Blair play.

Knock Knock.
Who's there?
Blood.
Blood who?
Blood brothers.

Knock Knock.
Who's there?
Blue.
Blue who?
Blue away with the wind.

Knock Knock.
Who's there?
Blur.
Blur who?
Blur! It's cold out here.

Knock Knock.
Who's there?
Bolton.
Bolton who?
Bolton braces.

Knock Knock.
Who's there?
Bones.
Bones who?
Bones upon a time . . .

Knock Knock.
Who's there?
Boo.
Boo who?
Oh please don't cry!

Knock Knock.
Who's there?
Borg.
Borg who?
Borg standard.

Knock Knock.
Who's there?
Bosnia.
Bosnia who?
Bosnia bell here earlier.

Knock Knock.
Who's there?
Bowl.
Bowl who?
Bowl me over.

Knock Knock.
Who's there?
Boyzone.
Boyzone who?
Boyzone adventures.

Knock Knock.
Who's there?
Brazil.
Brazil who?
Brazil hold your breasts up.

Knock Knock.
Who's there?
Bridget.
Bridget who?
Bridget the end of the world.

Knock Knock.
Who's there?
Brighton.
Brighton who?
Brightonder the light of the full moon.

Knock Knock.
Who's there?
Briony.
Briony who?
Briony, beautiful sea.

Knock Knock.
Who's there?
Brother.
Brother who?
Brotheration! I've forgotten my own name!

Knock Knock.
Who's there?
Bug.
Bug who?
Bug Rogers.

Knock Knock.
Who's there?
Bull.
Bull who?
Bull the chain.

Knock Knock.
Who's there?
Burglar.
Burglar who?
Burglars don't knock.

Knock Knock.
Who's there?
Buster.
Buster who?
Buster blood vessel.

Knock Knock.
Who's there?
Butcher.
Butcher who?
Butcher left leg in, your left leg out . . .

Knock Knock.
Who's there?
Butter.
Butter who?
Butter wrap up – it's cold out here.

Knock Knock.
Who's there?
Caesar.
Caesar who?
Caesar arm to stop her getting away.

Knock knock.
Who's there?
Candace.
Candace who?
Candace be love?

Knock Knock.
Who's there?
Canoe.
Canoe who?
Canoe lend me some money.

Knock Knock.
Who's there?
Canon.
Canon who?
Canon open the door then.

Knock Knock.
Who's there?
Card.
Card who?
Card you see it's me!

Knock Knock.
Who's there?
Carlo.
Carlo who?
Carload of junk.

Knock Knock.
Who's there?
Carrie.
Carrie who?
Carrie on camping!

Knock Knock.
Who's there?
Cat.
Cat who?
Cat you understand?

Knock Knock.
Who's there?
Caterpillar.
Caterpillar who?
Caterpillar a few mice for you.

Knock Knock.
Who's there?
Cattle.
Cattle who?
Cattle purr if you stroke it.

Knock Knock.
Who's there?
Cecile.
Cecile who?
Cecile th-the w-windows. Th-there's a m-monster out there.

Knock Knock.
Who's there?
Cello.
Cello who?
Cello, how are you?

Knock Knock.
Who's there?
Census.
Census who?
Census presents for Christmas.

Knock Knock.
Who's there?
Cereal.
Cereal who?
Cereal pleasure to meet you.

Knock Knock.
Who's there?
Cheese.
Cheese who?
Cheese a jolly good fellow.

Knock Knock.
Who's there?
Cher.
Cher who?
Cher and share alike!

Knock Knock.
Who's there?
Chester.
Chester who?
Chester drawers.

Knock Knock.
Who's there?
Chicken.
Chicken who?
Chicken your pockets – I think your keys
are there.

Knock Knock.
Who's there?
Chile.
Chile who?
Chile without your coat on!

Knock Knock.
Who's there?
Chin and Tony.
Chin and Tony who?
Chin and Tonyk.

Knock Knock.
Who's there?
Chopin.
Chopin who?
Chopin the department store.

Knock Knock.
Who's there?
Chrysalis.
Chrysalis who?
Chrysalis the cake for you.

Knock Knock.
Who's there?
Churchill.
Churchill who?
Churchill be the best place for your
wedding.

Knock knock.
Who's there?
Clara.
Clara who?
Clara space on the table.

Knock Knock.
Who's there?
Clarence.
Clarence who?
Clarence Sale.

Knock Knock.
Who's there?
Claudette.
Claudette who?
Claudette a whole cake.

Knock Knock.
Who's there?
Clay.
Clay who?
Clay on, Sam.

Knock knock.
Who's there?
Cliff.
Cliff who?
Cliffhanger.

Knock Knock.
Who's there?
Clinton.
Clinton who?
Clinton your eye.

Knock Knock.
Who's there?
Coffin.
Coffin who?
Coffin and spluttering.

Knock Knock.
Who's there?
Cole.
Cole who?
Cole as a cucumber.

Knock Knock.
Who's there?
Colin.
Colin who?
Colin and see me next time you're passing.

Knock Knock.
Who's there?
Collie.
Collie who?
Collie Miss Molly, I don't know.

Knock Knock.
Who's there?
Congo.
Congo who?
Congo into the woods – it's dangerous.

Knock Knock.
Who's there?
Cookie.
Cookie who?
Cookien the kitchen – it's easier.

Knock Knock.
Who's there?
Corrinne.
Corrinne who?
Corrinne the bell now.

Knock Knock.
Who's there?
Cousin.
Cousin who?
Cousin stead of opening the door you're leaving me here.

Knock Knock.
Who's there?
Cream.
Cream who?
Cream louder so the police will come.

Knock Knock.
Who's there?
Crete.
Crete who?
Crete to see you.

Knock Knock.
Who's there?
Crock and Dial.
Crock and Dial who?
Crock and Dial Dundee.

Knock Knock.
Who's there?
Cuba.
Cuba who?
Cuba wood.

Knock Knock.
Who's there?
Curry.
Curry who?
Curry me all the way.

Knock Knock.
Who's there?
Cyprus.
Cyprus who?
Cyprus the bell?

Knock Knock.
Who's there?
Czech.
Czech who?
Czech before you open the door!

Knock Knock.
Who's there?
Daisy.
Daisy who?
Daisy that you are in, but I don't believe them.

Knock Knock.
Who's there?
Danielle.
Danielle who?
Danielle so loud, I heard you the first time.

Knock Knock.
Who's there?
Dave.
Dave who?
Dave-andalised our home.

Knock Knock.
Who's there?
De Niro.
De Niro who?
De Niro you get, the faster I run.

Knock Knock.
Who's there?
Debbie.
Debbie who?
Debbie or not to be.

Knock Knock.
Who's there?
Debussy.
Debussy who?
Debussy's never on time.

Knock Knock.
Who's there?
Delhi.
Delhi who?
Delhi a joke . . .

Knock Knock.
Who's there?
Delta.
Delta who?
Delta great hand of cards.

Knock Knock.
Who's there?
Denial.
Denial who?
Denial flows through Egypt.

Knock Knock.
Who's there?
Denmark.
Denmark who?
Denmark your own territory.

Knock Knock.
Who's there?
Depp.
Depp who?
Depp inside dear!

Knock knock.
Who's there?
Diana.
Diana who?
Diana thirst – a glass of water, please.

Knock Knock.
Who's there?
Diaz.
Diaz who?
Diaz of our lives.

Knock Knock.
Who's there?
Dickon.
Dickon who?
Dickon the right answer.

Knock Knock.
Who's there?
Diesel.
Diesel who?
Diesel make you feel better.

Knock Knock.
Who's there?
Dimaggio.
Dimaggio who?
Dimaggio yourself on a deserted island . . .

Knock Knock.
Who's there?
Disc.
Disc who?
Discusting!

Knock Knock.
Who's there?
Dish.
Dish who?
Dish ish a shtick-up!

Knock Knock.
Who's there?
Dishwasher.
Dishwasher who?
Dishwasher way I shpoke before I had my teef fixshed.

Knock Knock.
Who's there?
Dismay.
Dismay who?
Dismay surprise you but I'm from New York.

Knock Knock.
Who's there?
Distress.
Distress who?
Distress is brand new.

Knock Knock.
Who's there?
Doctor.
Doctor Who?
That's right – where's my Tardis?

Knock Knock.
Who's there?
Dolly.
Dolly who?
Dolly't us in, we're cold!

Knock Knock.
Who's there?
Donovan.
Donovan who?
Donovan the door – it's dangerous.

Knock Knock.
Who's there?
Doughnut.
Doughnut who?
Doughnut open the door whatever you do.

Knock knock.
Who's there?
Douglas.
Douglas who?
Douglas is broken.

Knock Knock.
Who's there?
Dozen.
Dozen who?
Dozen anyone know my name?

Knock Knock.
Who's there?
Drum.
Drum who?
Drum as fast as you can.

Knock Knock.
Who's there?
Dublin.
Dublin who?
Dublin up with laughter.

Knock Knock.
Who's there?
Duke.
Duke who?
Duke come here often?

Knock Knock.
Who's there?
Duncan.
Duncan who?
Duncan make your garden grow.

Knock Knock.
Who's there?
Dutch.
Dutch who?
Dutch me in the morning.

Knock Knock.
Who's there?
Ears.
Ears who?
Ears looking at you kid.

Knock Knock.
Who's there?
Earwig.
Earwig who?
Earwigo!

Knock Knock.
Who's there?
Edna.
Edna who?
Edna cloud.

Knock Knock.
Who's there?
Egg.
Egg who?
Eggsactly.

Knock Knock.
Who's there?
Egypt.
Egypt who?
Egypt me out in the cold!

Knock Knock.
Who's there?
Eileen.
Eileen who?
Eileen against the door.

Knock Knock.
Who's there?
Eisenhower.
Eisenhower who?
Eisenhower late for work.

Knock Knock.
Who's there?
Eli.
Eli who?
Elies all the time.

Knock Knock.
Who's there?
Ellen.
Ellen who?
Ellen all the ghouls are after me.

Knock Knock.
Who's there?
Elsie.
Elsie who?
Elsie you in court!

Knock Knock.
Who's there?
Emma.
Emma who?
Emma new neighbor – come round for tea.

Knock Knock.
Who's there?
Enid.
Enid who?
Enid some shelter from the ghouls.

Knock Knock.
Who's there?
Esau.
Esau who?
Esau you in the bath!

Knock Knock.
Who's there?
Ethan.
Ethan who?
Ethan people don't go to church.

Knock Knock.
Who's there?
Euripides.
Euripides who?
Euripides, you pay for a new pair.

Knock Knock.
Who's there?
Evan.
Evan who?
Evan you should know who it is.

Knock Knock.
Who's there?
Eve.
Eve who?
Eve-ho, here we go.

Knock Knock.
Who's there?
Evie.
Evie who?
Evie weather.

Knock knock.
Who's there?
Ewan.
Ewan who?
Ewan me should get together.

Knock knock.
Who's there?
Ezra.
Ezra who?
Ezra room to rent?

Knock Knock.
Who's there?
Fang.
Fang who?
Fangs for the memory.

Knock Knock.
Who's there?
Fanta.
Fanta who?
Fanta Claus.

Knock Knock.
Who's there?
Fantasy.
Fantasy who?
Fantasy a walk in the park?

Knock Knock.
Who's there?
Fax.
Fax who?
Fax you very much.

Knock knock.
Who's there?
Felicity.
Felicity who?
Felicity getting more polluted every day.

Knock Knock.
Who's there?
Felipe.
Felipe who?
Felipe bath – I need a wash!

Knock Knock.
Who's there?
Felix.
Felix who?
Felix his bottom again I'll scream!

Knock Knock.
Who's there?
Fergie.
Fergie who?
Fergiedness sake let me in!

Knock Knock.
Who's there?
Few.
Few who?
Few! What's that smell?

Knock Knock.
Who's there?
Fido.
Fido who?
Fido known you were coming I'd have
bolted all the doors.

Knock Knock.
Who's there?
Fig.
Fig who?
Figs the step, it's broken.

Knock Knock.
Who's there?
Fish.
Fish who?
Bless you!

Knock Knock.
Who's there?
Flea.
Flea who?
Flea blind mice.

Knock Knock.
Who's there?
Florida.
Florida who?
Florida room is sticky.

Knock Knock.
Who's there?
Fonda.
Fonda who?
Fonda my family.

Knock Knock.
Who's there?
Foot.
Foot who?
Foot two pence I'd go away now.

Knock Knock.
Who's there?
Fork.
Fork who?
Forket her – she wasn't worth it.

Knock Knock.
Who's there?
Francis.
Francis who?
Francis next to Germany.

Knock Knock.
Who's there?
Fred.
Fred who?
Fred I've got some bad news.

Knock Knock.
Who's there?
Freddie and Abel.
Freddie and Abel who?
Freddie and Abel to do business.

Knock Knock.
Who's there?
Fruit.
Fruit who?
Fruit of all evil.

Knock Knock.
Who's there?
Furry.
Furry who?
Furry's a jolly good fellow!

Knock knock.
Who's there?
Gail.
Gail who?
Gail of laughter.

Knock Knock.
Who's there?
Galway.
Galway who?
Galway you silly boy.

Knock Knock.
Who's there?
Gandhi.
Gandhi who?
Gandhi come out to play?

Knock Knock.
Who's there?
Gaskill.
Gaskill who?
Gaskills if it's not turned off.

Knock Knock.
Who's there?
Gazza.
Gazza who?
Gazza kiss.

Knock Knock.
Who's there?
Gerald.
Gerald who?
Gerald man from round the corner.

Knock Knock.
Who's there?
Ghent.
Ghent who?
Ghent out of town.

Knock Knock.
Who's there?
Ghoul.
Ghoul who?
Ghoulpost painter.

Knock Knock.
Who's there?
Giovanni.
Giovanni who?
Giovanniny more coffee?

Knock Knock.
Who's there?
Giuseppe.
Giuseppe who?
Giuseppe credit cards.

Knock Knock.
Who's there?
Glasgow.
Glasgow who?
Glasgow to the theater.

Knock Knock.
Who's there?
Gopher.
Gopher who?
Gopher help – I'm stuck in the mud.

Knock Knock.
Who's there?
Gorilla.
Gorilla who?
Gorilla sausage.

Knock Knock.
Who's there?
Grace.
Grace who?
Grace your knee.

Knock Knock.
Who's there?
Grapes.
Grapes who?
Grapes Suzette.

Knock Knock.
Who's there?
Gray.
Gray who?
Grayt balls of fire!

Knock Knock.
Who's there?
Greece.
Greece who?
Greece my palm and I'll tell you.

Knock Knock.
Who's there?
Grimm.
Grimm who?
Grimm and bear it.

Knock Knock.
Who's there?
Grub.
Grub who?
Grub hold of my hand and let's go!

Knock Knock.
Who's there?
Guinea.
Guinea who?
Guinea a high five!

Knock Knock.
Who's there?
Haden.
Haden who?
Haden in the bushes.

Knock Knock.
Who's there?
Hair.
Hair who?
Hair you go!

Knock Knock.
Who's there?
Haiti.
Haiti who?
Haitit when you talk like that!

Knock knock.
Who's there?
Hannah.
Hannah who?
Hannah cloth out to dry.

Knock Knock.
Who's there?
Hand.
Hand who?
Handover your money.

Knock Knock.
Who's there?
Handel.
Handel who?
Handel with care.

Knock Knock.
Who's there?
Hardy.
Hardy who?
Hardy annual.

Knock Knock.
Who's there?
Harlow.
Harlow who?
Harlow can you get?

Knock Knock.
Who's there?
Harp.
Harp who?
Harp the Herald Angels Sing!

Knock Knock.
Who's there?
Harrison.
Harrison who?
Harrison is a credit to his father.

Knock Knock.
Who's there?
Harry.
Harry who?
Harry up! There's a ghoul after us!

Knock Knock.
Who's there?
Havana.
Havana who?
Havana spooky old time!

Knock Knock.
Who's there?
Hawaii.
Hawaii who?
Hawaii getting on?

Knock Knock.
Who's there?
Haydn.
Haydn who?
Haydn the shed.

Knock Knock.
Who's there?
Heidi.
Heidi who?
Heidi hi campers!

Knock Knock.
Who's there?
Hester.
Hester who?
Hester la vista!

Knock Knock.
Who's there?
Heywood.
Heywood who?
Heywood you open the door?

Knock Knock.
Who's there?
Hip.
Hip who?
Hippopotamous.

Knock Knock.
Who's there?
Horn.
Horn who?
Horn the way home.

Knock Knock.
Who's there?
Hosanna.
Hosanna who?
Hosanna Claus gets down our tiny chimney
I'll never know!

Knock Knock.
Who's there?
House.
House who?
Hugh's fine thanks. How's John?

Knock Knock.
Who's there?
Howl.
Howl who?
Howl I know when it's supper time?

Knock knock.
Who's there?
Huey.
Huey who?
Who am I? I'm me!

Knock knock.
Who's there?
Hugh.
Hugh who?
Hugh wouldn't believe it if I told you.

Knock Knock.
Who's there?
Ice cream.
Ice cream who?
Ice cream loudly.

Knock Knock.
Who's there?
Ida.
Ida who?
Ida thought you could say please.

Knock knock.
Who's there?
Ina Claire.
Ina Claire who?
Ina Claire day you can see forever.

Knock Knock.
Who's there?
Insect.
Insect who?
Insect your name and address here.

Knock Knock.
Who's there?
Iowa.
Iowa who?
Iowa lot to you.

Knock Knock.
Who's there?
Iran.
Iran who?
Iran all the way here. Let me in!

Knock Knock.
Who's there?
Ivana.
Ivana who?
Ivana be alone.

Knock Knock.
Who's there?
Jagger.
Jagger who?
Jaggered edge.

Knock Knock.
Who's there?
Jam.
Jam who?
Jam mind! I'm trying to think out here.

Knock knock.
Who's there?
Janet.
Janet who?
Janet a big fish?

Knock knock.
Who's there?
Jasmine.
Jasmine who?
Jasmine like to play in bands.

Knock Knock.
Who's there?
Java.
Java who?
Java cat in your house?

Knock Knock.
Who's there?
Jaws.
Jaws who?
Jaws which one you want.

Knock Knock.
Who's there?
Jeanette.
Jeanette who?
Jeanette a big fish this time?

Knock Knock.
Who's there?
Jess.
Jess who?
Jess li'l ol' me.

Knock Knock.
Who's there?
Jester.
Jester who?
Jester silly old man.

Knock Knock.
Who's there?
Jewel.
Jewel who?
Jewel know me when you open the door.

Knock Knock.
Who's there?
Jez.
Jez who?
Jezt a minute.

Knock Knock.
Who's there?
Joan.
Joan who?
Joan you know your own daughter?

Knock Knock.
Who's there?
Joanna.
Joanna who?
Joanna smack, let me in.

Knock Knock.
Who's there?
Joplin.
Joplin who?
Joplin any time you like.

Knock Knock.
Who's there?
Juan.
Juan who?
Juance upon a time there were three bears . . .

Knock Knock.
Who's there?
Juana.
Juana who?
Juana go out with me?

Knock knock.
Who's there?
Juanita.
Juanita who?
Juanita big meal?

Knock Knock.
Who's there?
Juice.
Juice who?
Juice still want to know?

Knock Knock.
Who's there?
Juicy.
Juicy who?
Juicy what I see?

Knock Knock.
Who's there?
July.
July who?
July or do you tell the truth?

Knock Knock.
Who's there?
June.
June who?
Juneno what time it is?

Knock Knock.
Who's there?
Justine.
Justine who?
Justine the nick of time.

Knock Knock.
Who's there?
Karen.
Karen who?
Karen the can for you.

Knock Knock.
Who's there?
Keanu.
Keanu who?
Keanu let me in? It's cold out here.

Knock Knock.
Who's there?
Kent.
Kent who?
Kent see without my glasses.

Knock knock.
Who's there?
Ken.
Ken who?
Ken you come and play?

Knock Knock.
Who's there?
Kenya.
Kenya who?
Kenya guess?

Knock Knock.
Who's there?
Kermit.
Kermit who?
Kermit a crime and you go to jail.

Knock Knock.
Who's there?
Ketchup.
Ketchup who?
Ketchup the tree.

Knock Knock.
Who's there?
Kevin.
Kevin who?
Kevin it all you've got.

Knock Knock.
Who's there?
Khomeini.
Khomeini who?
Khomeini time you like.

Knock knock.
Who's there?
Kiki.
Kiki who?
Kiki's stuck in the lock – let me in.

Knock Knock.
Who's there?
Kipper.
Kipper who?
Kipper your hands to yourself.

Knock Knock.
Who's there?
Kismet.
Kismet who?
Kismet quick!

Knock Knock.
Who's there?
Knee.
Knee who?
Kneed you ask?

Knock Knock.
Who's there?
Knees.
Knees who?
Knees you every day.

Knock knock.
Who's there?
Kurt.
Kurt who?
Kurt and wounded.

Knock Knock.
Who's there?
Kylie.
Kylie who?
Kyliet your dog out for a walk?

Knock Knock.
Who's there?
Kyoto.
Kyoto who?
Kyoto the priest before the ghoulies get you.

Knock Knock.
Who's there?
Kyoto.
Kyoto who?
Kyoto town tonight!

Knock Knock.
Who's there?
Lara.
Lara who?
Lara lara laffs in Liverpool.

Knock Knock.
Who's there?
Larva.
Larva who?
Larva cup of coffee.

Knock Knock.
Who's there?
Leaf.
Leaf who?
Leaf me be!

Knock Knock.
Who's there?
Letter.
Letter who?
Letter in!

Knock Knock.
Who's there?
Lettuce.
Lettuce who?
Lettuce in and we'll tell you.

Knock knock.
Who's there?
Lily.
Lily who?
Lily livered varmint!

Knock Knock.
Who's there?
Linnekar.
Linnekar who?
Linnekars in a big traffic jam.

Knock Knock.
Who's there?
Lisa.
Lisa who?
Lisa'n life.

Knock Knock.
Who's there?
Little old lady.
Little old lady who?
I didn't know you could yodel.

Knock Knock.
Who's there?
Liz.
Liz who?
Lizen carefully, I will say this only once.

Knock Knock.
Who's there?
Lock.
Lock who?
Lock through the peephole.

Knock Knock.
Who's there?
Lolly.
Lolly who?
Lollyng about on the sofa.

Knock Knock.
Who's there?
Lulu.
Lulu who?
Lulu's not working, can I use yours?

Knock Knock.
Who's there?
Lumley.
Lumley who?
Lumley cakes!

Knock Knock.
Who's there?
Madrid.
Madrid who?
Madrid you wash my sports kit?

Knock Knock.
Who's there?
Maggot.
Maggot who?
Maggot me this new dress today.

Knock Knock.
Who's there?
Maia.
Maia who?
Maianimals are like children to me.

Knock Knock.
Who's there?
Major.
Major who?
Major answer the door didn't I?

Knock Knock.
Who's there?
Malt.
Malt who?
Maltesers the girls terribly.

Knock Knock.
Who's there?
Mamie.
Mamie who?
Mamie a new dress.

Knock Knock.
Who's there?
Manchu.
Manchu who?
Manchu your food six times.

Knock Knock.
Who's there?
Mandy.
Mandy who?
Mandy guns.

Knock Knock.
Who's there?
Mao.
Mao who?
Maothful of toffee.

Knock Knock.
Who's there?
Marcia.
Marcia who?
Marcia me!

Knock knock.
Who's there?
Maria.
Maria who?
Marial name is Mary.

Knock Knock.
Who's there?
Marie.
Marie who?
Marie me or I'll cast a spell on you.

Knock Knock.
Who's there?
Mars.
Mars who?
Marsays you've got to come home now.

Knock Knock.
Who's there?
Maude.
Maude who?
Maude of wood.

Knock Knock.
Who's there?
Mauve.
Mauve who?
Mauve over!

Knock Knock.
Who's there?
Max.
Max who?
Max Headroom.

Knock Knock.
Who's there?
Max.
Max who?
Maximum security is needed in these
parts.

Knock Knock.
Who's there?
McEnroe.
McEnroe who?
McEnroe fast with his own oar.

Knock Knock.
Who's there?
Me.
Me who?
I didn't know you had a cat!

Knock Knock.
Who's there?
Mecca.
Mecca who?
Mecca my day!

Knock Knock.
Who's there?
Megan.
Megan who?
Megan a cake.

Knock Knock.
Who's there?
Melon.
Melon who?
Melond Kim.

Knock Knock.
Who's there?
Mike and Angelo.
Mike and Angelo who?
Mike and Angelo's David.

Knock Knock.
Who's there?
Mike.
Mike who?
Mike-andle's just blown out. It's all dark.

Knock Knock.
Who's there?
Minsk.
Minsk who?
Minsk meat.

Knock Knock.
Who's there?
Mint.
Mint who?
Mint to tell you earlier.

Knock Knock.
Who's there?
Missouri.
Missouri who?
Missouri me! I'm so scared!

Knock Knock.
Who's there?
Miss Piggy.
Miss Piggy who?
Miss Piggy went to market, Miss Piggy
stayed at home . . .

Knock Knock.
Who's there?
Mom.
Mom who?
Mom's the word.

Knock Knock.
Who's there?
Money.
Money who?
Money is hurting – I knocked it playing
football.

Knock Knock.
Who's there?
Monster.
Monster who?
Monster munch.

Knock Knock.
Who's there?
Moscow.
Moscow who?
Moscow home soon.

Knock Knock.
Who's there?
Moses.
Moses who?
Moses the lawn.

Knock Knock.
Who's there?
Mosquito.
Mosquito who?
Mosquito smoking soon.

Knock Knock.
Who's there?
Moth.
Moth who?
Moth get mythelf a key.

Knock Knock.
Who's there?
Mountain.
Mountain who?
Mountain debts.

Knock Knock.
Who's there?
Muffin.
Muffin who?
Muffin to declare.

Knock Knock.
Who's there?
Munro.
Munro who?
Munro fast to the other side.

Knock Knock.
Who's there?
Murphy.
Murphy who?
Murphy, have murphy! Don't eat me!

Knock Knock.
Who's there?
Musketeer.
Musketeer who?
Musketeer a doorbell – I'm tired of
knocking.

Knock Knock.
Who's there?
Mustard.
Mustard who?
Mustard left it in the car.

Knock Knock.
Who's there?
Myth.
Myth who?
Myth Thmith thilly!

Knock Knock.
Who's there?
Nanny.
Nanny who?
Nanny people are waiting to come in.

Knock Knock.
Who's there?
Nanny.
Nanny who?
Nanny-one home?

Knock Knock.
Who's there?
Neil.
Neil who?
Neil down before the vampire king!

Knock Knock.
Who's there?
Nell.
Nell who?
Nell is hot.

Knock Knock.
Who's there?
Nestle.
Nestle who?
Nestle into the soft chair.

Knock Knock.
Who's there?
Ninja.
Ninja who?
Ninja with me every day.

Knock Knock.
Who's there?
Noah.
Noah who?
Noah counting for taste.

Knock Knock.
Who's there?
Nobody.
Nobody who?
Just nobody.

Knock Knock.
Who's there?
Noise.
Noise who?
Noise to see you.

Knock Knock.
Who's there?
Norway.
Norway who?
Norway is this your house – it's so big!

Knock Knock.
Who's there?
Nose.
Nose who?
Nosinging in the house.

Knock Knock.
Who's there?
Nougat.
Nougat who?
Nougat can go that fast!

Knock Knock.
Who's there?
Oboe.
Oboe who?
Oboe! I've got the wrong house!

Knock Knock.
Who's there?
Oil.
Oil who?
Oil be seeing you.

Knock Knock.
Who's there?
Olive.
Olive who?
Olive to regret.

Knock Knock.
Who's there?
Oliver.
Oliver who?
Oliver lone and I'm frightened of monsters.

Knock Knock.
Who's there?
Olivier.
Olivier who?
Olivier all my money in my will.

Knock knock.
Who's there?
Onya.
Onya who?
Onya marks, get set, go.

Knock Knock.
Who's there?
Opi.
Opi who?
Opi cushion.

Knock Knock.
Who's there?
Orange.
Orange who?
Orange your day to suit the weather.

Knock Knock.
Who's there?
Organ.
Organ who?
Organize a party – it's my birthday.

Knock Knock.
Who's there?
Orson.
Orson who?
Orson, let your daddy in.

Knock Knock.
Who's there?
Owl.
Owl who?
Owl be sad if you don't let me in.

Knock Knock.
Who's there?
Oz.
Oz who?
Oz got something for you.

Knock Knock.
Who's there?
Panther.
Panther who?
Panther what you wear on your legth.

Knock Knock.
Who's there?
Paris.
Paris who?
Paris by the vampire very quietly.

Knock Knock.
Who's there?
Parsley.
Parsley who?
Parsley jam please.

Knock Knock.
Who's there?
Panon.
Panon who?
Panon my intrusion.

Knock Knock.
Who's there?
Pasta.
Pasta who?
Pasta salt please.

Knock Knock.
Who's there?
Paul and Portia
Paul and Portia who?
Paul and Portia door to open it.

Knock Knock.
Who's there?
Paul.
Paul who?
Paul your weight!

Knock Knock.
Who's there?
Pear.
Pear who?
Pear of shoes.

Knock Knock.
Who's there?
Peas.
Peas who?
Peas to meet you.

Knock Knock.
Who's there?
Pecan.
Pecan who?
Pecan boo!

Knock Knock.
Who's there?
Pen.
Pen who?
Pent-up emotions!

Knock Knock.
Who's there?
Pencil.
Pencil who?
Pencil fall down if your belt snaps.

Knock Knock.
Who's there?
Pepsi.
Pepsi who?
Pepsi through the peephole.

Knock knock.
Who's there?
Percy.
Percy who?
Percy Verence is the secret of success.

Knock knock.
Who's there?
Perry.
Perry who?
Perry well, thank you.

Knock Knock.
Who's there?
Perth.
Perth who?
Perth full of money.

Knock Knock.
Who's there?
Peru.
Peru who?
Peruse this map before you go.

Knock Knock.
Who's there?
Peter.
Peter who?
Peter cake.

Knock Knock.
Who's there?
Philippa.
Philippa who?
Philippa a bath – I'm really dirty.

Knock Knock.
Who's there?
Phone.
Phone who?
Phone I'd known it was you.

Knock Knock.
Who's there?
Piano.
Piano who?
Piano Ferries.

Knock Knock.
Who's there?
Pill.
Pill who?
Pill you open the door?

Knock Knock.
Who's there?
Pizza.
Pizza who?
Pizza this, piece of that.

Knock Knock.
Who's there?
Plums.
Plums who?
Plums me you won't tell.

Knock Knock.
Who's there?
Police.
Police who?
Police open the door.

Knock knock.
Who's there?
Poppy.
Poppy who?
Poppy'n any time you like.

Knock Knock.
Who's there?
Posie.
Posie who?
Posie hard questions.

Knock Knock.
Who's there?
Pudding.
Pudding who?
Pudding our best feet forward.

Knock Knock.
Who's there?
Puss.
Puss who?
Puss the door – it won't open.

Knock Knock.
Who's there?
Python.
Python who?
Python with your pocket money.

Knock Knock.
Who's there?
Quebec.
Quebec who?
Quebec there, if you want a ticket.

Knock Knock.
Who's there?
Queen.
Queen who?
Queen of the crop.

Knock knock.
Who's there?
Ralph.
Ralph who?
Ralph, ralph – I'm just a puppy.

Knock knock.
Who's there?
Raoul.
Raoul who?
Raoul of law.

Knock Knock.
Who's there?
Rattlesnake.
Rattlesnake who?
Rattlesnake a big difference!

Knock Knock.
Who's there?
Ray.
Ray who?
Rayning cats and dogs.

Knock knock.
Who's there?
Raymond.
Raymond who?
Raymond me to take that book back.

Knock Knock.
Who's there?
Razor.
Razor who?
Razor laugh at that joke.

Knock Knock.
Who's there?
Red.
Red who?
Red any good books lately?

Knock knock.
Who's there?
Reuben.
Reuben who?
Reuben my eyes.

Knock knock.
Who's there?
Richard.
Richard who?
Richard poor have little in common.

Knock Knock.
Who's there?
Ringo.
Ringo who?
Ringof truth.

Knock Knock.
Who's there?
Rio
Rio who?
Riorrange your appointment please.

Knock Knock.
Who's there?
Roach.
Roach who?
Roach out and touch somebody.

Knock knock.
Who's there?
Robin.
Robin who?
Robin banks.

Knock Knock.
Who's there?
Roland.
Roland who?
Roland stone gathers no moss.

Knock Knock.
Who's there?
Ron.
Ron who?
Ron answer.

Knock Knock.
Who's there?
Rosie.
Rosie who?
Rosie-lee is the best cuppa in the morning.

Knock Knock.
Who's there?
Rothschild.
Rothschild who?
Rothschild is very clever.

Knock Knock.
Who's there?
Roxie.
Roxie who?
Roxie Horror Show.

Knock Knock.
Who's there?
Royal.
Royal who?
Royal show you his paintings if you ask nicely.

Knock knock.
Who's there?
Rudi.
Rudi who?
Rudi toot!

Knock Knock.
Who's there?
Russia.
Russia who?
Russia down the shops before they close.

Knock Knock.
Who's there?
Ryder.
Ryder who?
Ryder fast horse.

Knock Knock.
Who's there?
Sacha.
Sacha who?
Sacha money in the bank.

Knock Knock.
Who's there?
Saddam.
Saddam who?
Saddam I that you couldn't come to the party.

Knock knock.
Who's there?
Sam.
Sam who?
Sam day you'll recognize my voice.

Knock Knock.
Who's there?
Scargill.
Scargill who?
Scargill not go any faster.

Knock Knock.
Who's there?
Scold.
Scold who?
Scold outside. Please let me in.

Knock Knock.
Who's there?
Scott.
Scott who?
Scott land the brave.

Knock Knock.
Who's there?
Scully.
Scully who?
Scully-wag!

Knock knock.
Who's there?
Sebastian.
Sebastian who?
Sebastian of society.

Knock Knock.
Who's there?
Serpent.
Serpent who?
Serpents are working hard, sir.

Knock Knock.
Who's there?
Seville.
Seville who?
Seville Row suit.

Knock knock.
Who's there?
Seymour.
Seymour who?
Seymour from the top window.

Knock Knock.
Who's there?
Sheik and Geisha.
Sheik and Geisha who?
Sheik and Geisha'll find.

Knock Knock.
Who's there?
Sherlock.
Sherlock who?
Sherlock your door – someone could break in.

Knock Knock.
Who's there?
Shields.
Shields who?
Shields say anything.

Knock Knock.
Who's there?
Shoes.
Shoes who?
Shoes me, I didn't mean to steal your
pears.

Knock Knock.
Who's there?
Sienna.
Sienna who?
Siennathing good at the movies.

Knock Knock.
Who's there?
Sigrid.
Sigrid who?
Sigrid Service.

Knock Knock.
Who's there?
Sloane.
Sloane who?
Sloanely outside - let me in.

Knock Knock.
Who's there?
Smarties.
Smarties who?
Smartiest kid in the class.

Knock Knock.
Who's there?
Smee.
Smee who?
Smee, your friend.

Knock Knock.
Who's there?
Snow.
Snow who?
Snow business of yours.

Knock Knock.
Who's there?
Sondheim.
Sondheim who?
Sondheim soon we'll meet again.

Knock Knock.
Who's there?
Sophia.
Sophia who?
Sophia nothing . . . fear is pointless.

Knock Knock.
Who's there?
Sorrel.
Sorrel who?
Sorrel about the mess.

Knock Knock.
Who's there?
Soup.
Soup who?
Souper Mom!

Knock Knock.
Who's there?
Spice.
Spice who?
Spice satellites are orbiting the earth.

Knock Knock.
Who's there?
Spider.
Spider who?
Spider through the keyhole.

Knock Knock.
Who's there?
Spider.
Spider who?
Spider when she thought I wasn't looking.

Knock Knock.
Who's there?
Spock.
Spock who?
Spocken like a true gentleman.

Knock Knock.
Who's there?
Stalin.
Stalin who?
Stalin for time.

Knock Knock.
Who's there?
Stan and Della.
Stan and Della who?
Stan and Dellaver.

Knock Knock.
Who's there?
Stones.
Stones who?
Stones sober.

Knock Knock.
Who's there?
Street.
Street who?
Street to go out to dinner.

Knock Knock.
Who's there?
Summer.
Summer who?
Summer good, some are bad.

Knock Knock.
Who's there?
Sweden.
Sweden who?
Sweden the pill.

Knock Knock.
Who's there?
Tango.
Tango who?
Tango faster than this you know.

Knock Knock.
Who's there?
Tarzan.
Tarzan who?
Tarzan stripes forever!

Knock Knock.
Who's there?
Teheran.
Teheran who?
Teheran very slowly – there's a monster behind you.

Knock Knock.
Who's there?
Teheran.
Teheran who?
Teheran and look me in the eye.

Knock Knock.
Who's there?
Telly.
Telly who?
Telly your friend to come out.

Knock Knock.
Who's there?
Tennis.
Tennis who?
Tennis five plus five.

Knock Knock.
Who's there?
Termite.
Termite who?
Termite's the night!

Knock Knock.
Who's there?
Thea.
Thea who?
Thea later alligator.

Knock Knock.
Who's there?
Theresa.
Theresa who?
Theresa green.

Knock Knock.
Who's there?
Thighs.
Thighs who?
Thighs the limit.

Knock Knock.
Who's there?
Thistle.
Thistle who?
Thistle be the last time I knock.

Knock Knock.
Who's there?
Throat.
Throat who?
Throat to me.

Knock Knock.
Who's there?
Thumb.
Thumb who?
Thumb like it hot.

Knock Knock.
Who's there?
Thumping.
Thumping who?
Thumping green and slimy is creeping up
your leg.

Knock Knock.
Who's there?
Tic tac.
Tic tac who?
Tic tac paddy whack, give the dog a bone.

Knock Knock.
Who's there?
Tick.
Tick who?
Tick 'em up and gimme all your money.

Knock Knock.
Who's there?
Tilly.
Tilly who?
Tilly learns to say please, he'll stay
outside.

Knock Knock.
Who's there?
Toffee.
Toffee who?
Toffeel loved is the best feeling in the
world.

Knock Knock.
Who's there?
Too whit.
Too whit who?
Is there an owl in the house?

Knock Knock.
Who's there?
Tooth.
Tooth who?
Tooth or dare.

Knock Knock.
Who's there?
Topic.
Topic who?
Topic a wild flower is against the law.

Knock Knock.
Who's there?
Toto.
Toto who?
Totolly devoted to you.

Knock Knock.
Who's there?
Tristan.
Tristan who?
Tristan insect to really get up your nose.

Knock Knock.
Who's there?
Truffle.
Truffle who?
Truffle with you is you are so shy.

Knock Knock.
Who's there?
Tubby.
Tubby who?
Tubby or not to be.

Knock Knock.
Who's there?
Tummy.
Tummy who?
Tummy you'll always be the best.

Knock Knock.
Who's there?
Tuna.
Tuna who?
Tuna whole orchestra.

Knock Knock.
Who's there?
Turin.
Turin who?
Turin to a werewolf under a full moon.

Knock Knock.
Who's there?
Turner.
Turner who?
Turner round, there's a monster breathing down your neck.

Knock Knock.
Who's there?
Twix.
Twix who?
Twixt you and me there's a lot of love.

Knock Knock.
Who's there?
Twyla.
Twyla who?
Twylight of your life.

Knock Knock.
Who's there?
Tyson.
Tyson who?
Tyson of this for size.

Knock Knock.
Who's there?
UB40.
UB40 who?
UB40 today – happy birthday!

Knock Knock.
Who's there?
Uganda.
Uganda who?
Uganda go away now.

Knock Knock.
Who's there?
Una.
Una who?
Yes, Una who.

Knock Knock.
Who's there?
Underwear.
Underwear who?
Underwear my baby is tonight?

Knock Knock.
Who's there?
Vault.
Vault who?
Vaultsing Matilda.

Knock Knock.
Who's there?
Venice.
Venice who?
Venice this going to end?

Knock Knock.
Who's there?
Verdi.
Verdi who?
Verdia want to go?

Knock Knock.
Who's there?
Vic.
Vic who?
Victim of a vampire.

Knock Knock.
Who's there?
Vincent.
Vincent who?
Vincent alive anymore.

Knock Knock.
Who's there?
Violin.
Violin who?
Violin horrible boy.

Knock Knock.
Who's there?
Viper.
Viper who?
Viper your nose!

Knock Knock
Who's there?
Voodoo.
Voodoo who?
Voodoo you think you are?

Knock Knock.
Who's there?
Walter.
Walter who?
Walter wall.

Knock Knock.
Who's there?
Ward.
Ward who?
Ward you want?

Knock Knock.
Who's there?
Watson.
Watson who?
Watson your head, it looks silly?

Knock Knock.
Who's there?
Webster.
Webster who?
Webster Spin, your friendly neighborhood
spider.

Knock Knock.
Who's there?
Weevil.
Weevil who?
Weevil work it out.

Knock Knock.
Who's there?
Weevil.
Weevil who?
Weevil make you talk.

Knock knock.
Who's there?
Wendy.
Wendy who?
Wendy come to take you away
I won't stop them!

Knock Knock.
Who's there?
White.
White who?
White in the middle of it.

Knock Knock.
Who's there?
Whitny.
Whitny who?
Whitnyssed the crime.

Knock Knock.
Who's there?
Wicked.
Wicked who?
Wicked make beautiful music together.

Knock Knock.
Who's there?
Wilfred.
Wilfred who?
Wilfred come if we ask nicely?

Knock Knock.
Who's there?
Witch.
Witch who?
Witch witch would you like it to be?

Knock Knock.
Who's there?
Wizard.
Wizard who?
Wizard you I'm lost.

Knock Knock.
Who's there?
Wooden shoe.
Wooden shoe who?
Wooden shoe like to know?

Knock Knock.
Who's there?
Woodworm.
Woodworm who?
Woodworm cake be enough or would you
like two?

Knock Knock.
Who's there?
Worm.
Worm who?
Worm in here isn't it?

Knock Knock.
Who's there?
Yellow.
Yellow who?
Yellowver the din – I can't hear you.

Knock Knock.
Who's there?
Yoga.
Yoga who?
Yoga what it takes!

Knock Knock.
Who's there?
You.
You who?
Who's that calling out?

Knock Knock.
Who's there?
Zippy.
Zippy who?
Zippydidooda, zippydeeay!